UNIVERSITY OF CALIFORNIA PUBLICATIONS
IN
AMERICAN ARCHAEOLOGY AND ETHNOLOGY

A MISSION RECORD OF THE CALIFORNIA INDIANS

From a Manuscript in the Bancroft Library.

BY

A. L. KROEBER.

In 1811 the Spanish viceregal government of Mexico sent to Alta California a list of questions regarding the Indians at the missions, their customs and disposition in their native state, and their condition under missionary influence. This "interrogatorio" was answered at the various missions, the replies collected, and prefaced by the president of the missions with a short general statement or abstract of the answers received to each question. The compilation was presumably forwarded to Mexico, and a copy retained in the Archives of the mission Santa Barbara. There a copy was made in 1877 by E. F. Murray for Mr. H. H. Bancroft. On the acquisition of the Bancroft Library by the University of California, this copy became available for study. Through the courtesy of Professor Henry Morse Stephens, and the Commission on the Bancroft Library, the writer is enabled to present the following translation of extracts from this document.[1]

---

[1] The copy at the University of California is in the Archives of the Mission Santa Barbara, Miscellaneous Papers, volume VII, beginning at page 112, as this series of documents is at present bound and paged, and is entitled: *Contestacion al Interrogatorio del año de 1811 por el Presidente de las Misiones de esta Alta California, y los Padres de la Misiones de San Miguel, San Antonio, Soledad,* etc. The heading of the document itself is: *Interrogatorio dirigido al Il^{mo} Sor Obispo de Sonora, a 6 de Octubre del año 1811, por el Exmo S^{or} Dⁿ Ciriaco Gonzales Carvajal, S^{rio} inter^o de la gobernacion del Reyno de Ultramar, y circulado por mi, de orⁿ del S^{or} Bⁿ Dⁿ José Joaquin Calvo, Gobernador de la expresada sagrada Mitra, y de los padres ministros de las misiones de San Miguel,* etc.

In the original, the various statements are not arranged primarily according to missions, but under the questions of the interrogatorio to which they are replies. A geographical order is however more convenient for ethnological uses and is here followed. The replies vary much in length, spirit, and value. Some of the missionaries evidently regarded compliance with the instructions of the questionnaire as an official requirement which was perfunctorily performed. In many cases no answers were given various questions at certain of the missions. Other fathers wrote more fully, but were more interested in the condition of the converted Indians than in their wild brethren or the customs of their fathers. Some, in answering those questions of the list that an ethnologist would be specially interested in, display lack of knowledge, for the replies are brief or vague and general; but others, notably the fathers at San Luis Rey, San Fernando, and San Carlos, show an exactness of knowledge that argues not only a long acquaintance but an interest in the Indian as such. It is of such replies that the extracts here given largely consist. They are only a minor part of the entire document. Other passages, dealing with the converted Indians, belong more properly to the realm of the historian of the missions than of the ethnologist; and the remainder would be of no great interest to either. In regard to what is presented, it must be admitted that many of the replies from different missions are practical duplications, and that but few are answered as a modern ethnologist would answer them; but all are truthful, some discriminating, and few prejudiced; and above all we have here, put down by observers on the spot more than eighty years ago, what the best ethnologist of today could not obtain more than fragments or traces of. Back of San Diego and San Luis Rey there are still Indians who preserve memory of the past; but in the remainder of the mission region, from San Juan Capistrano to San Francisco, the Indians are gone, nearly gone, or civilized and Christianized into a state of oblivion of ancient customs and beliefs. How little that is specific do we know of the Chumash and Costanoan and Esselen Indians! How much less of those of Salinan stock, whose former life has vanished with scarcely a trace! It is for this reason that these replies of the Franciscan fathers, however unconnected, and however incomplete, are of value.

The Spanish of some of the missionaries was not always above reproach. They used provincialisms and terms now obsolete. Their spelling was at times more phonetic than orthographic, and hasty punctuation has made some interminable sentences. One and all they wrote as they thought, simply, truthfully, and without regard to style. The copyist, or several, through whose hands their unvarnished statements are at present preserved at the University, have evidently at times added to the difficulties of the manuscript and contributed their share toward an occasional sentence that it is hard to make much sense of. Thanks are due Professor J. T. Clark for assistance in unravelling some of the more difficult passages.

The Bancroft Library is without a systematic catalogue, and it has not yet been possible to provide any arrangement by which a given work or volume can be readily found at will. This condition renders it difficult to use the many valuable books in the Library, and almost impossible to carry on extended work with the still more valuable manuscripts. There is little doubt that the Library contains among its buried treasures a number of unpublished manuscripts that will prove to be of importance to the ethnology of California and the Pacific Coast. It is hoped that the present contribution may stimulate interest in this important collection, and may call attention to the larger opportunities for the increase of knowledge that will be furnished when it shall be possible to equip the Library with that indispensable key to its usefulness that at present it lacks—a complete catalogue.

San Diego.[2]

The language which the Indians of this mission speak is the

---

[2] The replies made to the interrogatory from San Diego were probably received too late to be incorporated with the other reports, for they are found separate in another part of the Archives, volume III, page 27, of the Miscellaneous Papers. The fathers in charge of San Diego about 1814 were Fernando Martin and Jose Sanchez, according to Engelhardt's Franciscans in California, from which the data of a similar nature given below are also taken.

San Diego is the southernmost of the Franciscan missions of Upper California, the earliest founded, and the only one in the territory of the Yuman linguistic stock. From it are named the Diegueños, or Yuman Mission Indians, who survive today to the number of several hundred.

Man dialect. It is so called because they say faâ for yes and man for no.[3]

They have a great desire to assemble at a ceremony regarding a bird called vulture (gavilan). This ceremony begins with a search anxiously made for this bird, and they invite one another to seek it. This arises from the fact that there are at the mission certain keen neophytes, who, however, are lazy when it comes to work, such as gathering the seeds on which they live. Desiring to have what they can feast with, these have made use of the opportunity of hunting the said bird in order to seduce the more simple-minded ones. They tell them that this bird is a person, who can free them from their enemies and bestow upon them whatever they ask of him. However false this belief, they hold to it with great pertinacity, wherefore they cherish the bird with as much care as the best mother could show for her son. As soon as they have captured it, they bring it the best of what they have obtained in the hunt and in their food gathering. When it is well nourished, and grown, they kill it, and for its funeral they burn it. While it is in the bonfire, those who have assembled offer to it seeds, beads, and whatever they esteem most. In the following year they search for another vulture, and do the same with it. The means which has been found for separating them from these follies, is to set some good Indians to watch, and to chastise severely and in public those who gather for the occasion.[4]

Although this land is favored with many medicinal herbs, they do not use them nor did they ever use them.[5] There are certain

---

[3] This designation of the language does not appear to have survived. The Diegueño word for yes is e, or khan, good, and for no, umau or arkhamau. Man should therefore probably be read Mau. The sound f does not occur in the Yuman languages.

[4] Drastic; but if we remember that it was not the fathers' business to sympathize with the Indian's civilization or to study it, but to bring him, for his own supposed good, to another way of living and thinking, our censure will not be severe, however such practices conflict with modern principles. The bird, as among the neighboring Luiseño, is more probably the eagle than the California condor, which the word gavilan properly indicates; the ceremony is an annual one, common to most of the Mission Indians of Southern California, and held in memory of the dead. The San Luis Rey report describes the ceremony more fully.

[5] This is probably an extreme statement, but it is well known that Indian medicine depends far more on ceremonial or shamanistic practices, such as the sucking described below, than on any pharmaceutical remedies.

neophytes who are sagacious but very bad workers.[6] These persuade the others that they can cure them. Such are called guisyay, that is to say, wizard. Their method of doctoring is this. When they know that someone is sick, the patient goes to the cusiyay[7] or his relatives call him. This one takes in his mouth a stick or piece of wood or skin. He turns to the part of the body which is in pain and begins to draw and suck it. When he removes his mouth, he shows to the patient what he has been carrying in it, persuading him that it was this which hurt him. With this the patient remains much calmed and contented, believing that he is already free from his sickness. From this it is to be inferred that their greatest physical infirmity, and that which most destroys them, is melancholy or fear;[8] but the most common illness among them is venereal sickness.[9] Since four years there have been more deaths than baptisms. In this last year of 1814 the dead numbered one hundred and eighteen, those baptized seventy-five, adult pagans baptized being included in the latter number.

They are exceedingly desirous (apasionados) of preserving the customs of their elders.[10] They say that they came to these lands from the north.[11]

They do not observe any ceremony in their funerals. All that they do, and that by the affected indifference of the missionaries, is to throw some seeds in the shroud of the dead. They do this with loud weeping, which they keep up for some days.

---

[6] It will be seen that the father has a fondness for giving this explanation of Indian religious practices that meet his disapproval.

[7] Probably the same as guisyay above. The word has been obtained as kwisiayu by the author.

[8] An interesting confirmation of an opinion held by many ethnologists regarding most people that are primitive.

[9] Needless to say, derived from the whites. The virulence of this disease among the Indians would be sufficient evidence of its newness to them, even if this fact were not confirmed by general contemporary statement.

[10] The Indians of Yuman family probably show this trait more strongly than any others in California.

[11] The common tradition of the Indians of Southern California, except the Mohave, who derive their first origin from the west. The Indians of Lower California are also said to have believed that they came from the north.

The Indians (indiada) are much inclined to pride and rancor. The men pursue one another with death for jealousies and other vexations. When the women are angry with their husbands, or these have become attached to other women, they revenge themselves for their injuries by depriving themselves of life.[12]

No other idolatry is found among them than the vulture ceremony which has been described. The rite which they use in their funerals is to burn the body. While it is blazing, they throw seeds on the fire and cry out to the accompaniment of floods of tears, which may continue for days or even months.[13]

These Indians do not have, nor did they have, any musical instruments, except a sonajilta (timbrel) of a disagreeable sound.[14]

San Luis Rey.

The language of this mission is called Lamancus.[15]

Fights arise over any sort of trifle, and they readily kill one another.

---

[12] Suicide among many Indians is most frequent among women disappointed in love.

[13] Cremation was the mode of disposing of the dead in vogue, at the time of discovery and settlement, among the Indians of Lower California and all of southern Upper California except the Chumash. Numerous burials have been found in Santa Barbara and Ventura counties, and on the Santa Barbara islands; but from about Los Angeles south, and eastward across the state, the scarcity of human remains is such as to be conclusive evidence of the prevalence of cremation, even were the confirmatory evidence of observers lacking. Under mission influence, of course, graves soon replaced the funeral pyre.

[14] Drums are not known from Southern California, though baskets were sometimes beaten or scraped. Rattles were of turtle-shell or gourd.

[15] With San Luis Rey we enter Shoshonean territory, in which the three following missions were also situated. The Luiseño are the only group of California Indians besides the Diegueño to have been brought under mission control and to survive in any numbers. The account here given is probably from the pen of Father Antonio Peyri, who was for many years identified with San Luis Rey. Father Geronimo Boscana, author of the important account of the religion and customs of the neighboring San Jaun Capistrano Indians (in A. Robinson, Life in California, 1846), was at San Luis Rey from 1812 to 1813. The name Lamancus is not known. The only native name ordinarily given for this language, or the allied dialect of San Juan Capistrano, is Ne-tela, my speech, or Cham-tela, our speech.

They throw seeds, beads, and other objects into the fire in which they burn their dead.

We have not observed any other idolatry among these Indians than that connected with certain birds which they call azuts, which really are a kind of very large vulture.[16] At the right time, while still small, they take them from the nest (according to what they say there are never more than two), and he who has captured them presents them with many carabanas to the chief of the village. The chief raises them with much attention and care until they are grown up; when, being of good size, the Indians make their great festival with the following ceremonies.

The night before the festival they put the azuts or vultures in the middle of a large circle of themselves. While they dance and sing a very miste song, and while old men and old women are blowing out towards all points of the compass, and making a thousand strange faces and grimaces, they very slowly kill the birds. When they are dead, they extinguish the fire and all break out in wails, shouts, and outcries, as if they were crazy, waving firebrands and striking blows as if they were furious, in such a way as to cause horror and confusion. After a considerable space of time during which this extravagance lasts, they again light (atizar) the fire. They skin the birds and throw their flesh on the fire. Meanwhile they begin to sing again, and with somewhat more suavity. They keep the feathers of the birds with much escovra and veneration until the following day, when they make a sort of skirt of them. This skirt they put on a boy during the days that the ceremony lasts. Wearing this skirt, he dances in

---

[16] Azuts are really not vultures, that is, condors, but eagles. Ashwut is Luiseño for eagle, yungavaiwot for condor. The author's Luiseño and Diegueño informants always mentioned the eagle as the bird connected with this ceremony. Boscana, however, describes the bird as much resembling the common buzzard, but larger, which clearly makes it the condor. It is not unlikely that both species were used. The annual eagle ceremony, the central feature of which is the slow pressing to death of an eagle in the course of the night, has already been mentioned as one form of mourning ritual practiced by most of the mission tribes of Southern California. Boscana, in the dialect of San Juan Capistrano, calls both ceremony and bird panes. The dance in the eagle-feather skirt, paelt, Luiseño palat, is also described by Boscana. A Luiseño dance made in remembrance of a chief, in which one man wearing the palat dances alone, is called Morahash. The boys here described as wearing the eagle-feather skirt were probably initiates of the puberty ceremonials.

the middle of a great circle of Indians, who make turns (dan vueltas, make short excursions) in time to the measure to which the boy is dancing in the center. They make this dance at intervals, and other boys who have been assigned to this take the place of the first boy. After the ceremony the chief of the village keeps the skirts with great veneration or a species of idolatry. We made the most careful efforts to ascertain the purpose of this ritual, but we have never been able to extract anything else than that thus their ancestors made it.

In order to win in their games of obligations (empeño) they drink a liquid which they call mani, made from the root of toloache pounded and mixed with water.[17] This drink renders them inebriated, and at times they give forth what they have in the stomach. In the state of intelligence, from which they depart with this nonsense, they say that because the other fasted and drank more.[18]

These Indians do not use any sort of unusual drink, other than that made from toloache or mani. This drink does them so much damage, that if they drink a quantity, and do not vomit, they die in their intoxication, foaming at the mouth.

---

[17] The drinking of *Datura meteloides*, the common jimson-weed, Spanish toloache, is the most important act of an initiation ceremony for boys, held formerly by probably all the Indians of California that today are known as Mission Indians. A somewhat similar ceremony is practiced by the Yokuts Indians of the southern San Joaquin valley. The Mohave and Chumash used the plant for religious purposes, but are not known to have employed it specifically in connection with an initiation ceremony. The religious importance of jimson-weed among the Indians of Southern California, may be judged from the fact that almost all their public rituals are either mourning ceremonies, or puberty initiation ceremonies related to this one. The effect of jimson-weed is sometimes loosely compared to that of alcohol, but differs in that it quickly produces unconsciousness and visions, and if taken in excess not infrequently causes death, as our missionary informant states. In the jimson-weed ceremony the young men received knowledge of the religious beliefs and practices of their tribe. The plant was also used as a medicine, especially in the case of broken bones. The Cahuilla say that it was taken by them for practical motives like that here mentioned, namely, to become rich and be successful in worldly matters. The plant is called mani, manit, or manich by all the Shoshoneans of Southern California, except the Cahuilla, who name it kiksawal.

[18] The manuscript reading is confused here, apparently through an omission: cuya bevida los pone ebrios y veces provocan quanto tienen en el estomago, en la inteligencia, que se con este disparate pierden, dicen que porque el otro ayunó y bevió mas.

When there is an eclipse of the sun or of the moon they shout with very loud outcries, making noises by clapping their hands and in other ways. On being asked the reason, they have always answered us that they believe that an animal was trying to eat the sun or the moon, and that they did these extreme things in order to frighten him, thinking that if he ate them they would all perish.[19]

The method observed by these Indians in their illnesses is as follows: For external matters, such as wounds, they make a tight bandage above the wound, with the end that the illness may not go up higher. In addition they most commonly use one of the following remedies: a plaster of tule leaves, which they call pibut, cooked and chewed; at other times they use the wild onion, queheyaguis, chewed and made into a plaster. There is another herb which occurs on the seashore. This they burn and put the ashes on the wound. We do not know the name of this plant, but they call it chaeca. If the wound is a burn (quemadosa) they follow the same treatment as regards the ligature, but in addition they put on powdered prickly pear (tuna) leaves, naboi, or more often powdered excrement of the jackrabbit or rabbit, tosoyat posa. Others use leaves of sage (salvia), cosil. If the trouble is the bite of a poisonous animal, they use, again in addition to the ligature, a stone similar to lapis, xaclul. This stone they soak in the mouth, and when it has become wet they apply some of the moisture to the wound. They do the same for wounds from poisoned arrows. If the sickness is a swelling, they still do not forget the ligature, and in addition anoint with ointment or oil of the seed of the gourd (chilicote), ennuix, until it rabierta or esparrama. In the case of internal illnesses they tie up very tight the part of the body which most hurts them, which we have observed to be most commonly the capa. They use also certain powdered roots, which they drink mixed with water and with the following: the root of the mangle (mangrove?), hechis; of the elder (sahuco), crita; of the wild rose of Castile, husla; of wild

---

[19] Compare the same statement below regarding the San Juan Capistrano Indians, and what Boscana says on page 298. Compare also the prayer or formula sung by the Tachi Yokuts at an eclipse of the sun, present series, II, 374.

cane, hiquix; and of the plant called hial.[20] They say that these drinks are all purgatives, and the root of the mangle also very provocative to vomiting. They do not make use of blood-letting. They have certain doctors (curanderos), who suck the sick person wherever he feels most pain, and presently they extract from the mouth blood, or sometimes pebbles, sticks, bones, or bits of skin, which they have deceitfully provided themselves with before. Making the patient believe that this was the sickness, they presently blow towards the four winds, and the sick man remains well satisfied, although sicker than before. They make him keep diet so rigorously that ordinarily they do not give him anything to eat unless he asks for it. They also practice the superstitions of dances, songs, and breathings for the sick, while a wizard makes a thousand faces over him. Thus, when the first remedies do not avail, and one of these medicine-men is employed, he does not give over until he has killed the patient and made of him a martyr to the demon. In short, in the matter of their superstitions regarding sickness, idolatry, and witchcraft, they are so rare (raros), full of deceit, and reserved, that although I have been among them since the foundation of this mission, that which I can most readily manifest regarding these matters, is my ignorance of them. They never confess more than what they cannot deny.

They have an idea of a rational soul, which they call chamson, and believe that when they die this goes below to tolmar,[21] where all come together and live forever in much happiness. With this they have, however, no idea of reward or punishment.[22]

---

[20] The Luiseño dictionary of P. S. Sparkman gives pivut, a rush, *Juncus mertensianus*; kashil, white sage; navut, prickly pear; enwish, chilicothe, *Echinocystis macrocarpa*; kutpat, elder; ushla, wild rose; huikish, *Elymus condensatus*, a species of cane used for arrows.

[21] Chamson means "our heart," from cham-, the possessive prefix of the first person plural, and -sun or -shun, heart. The analogous term nu-shun was given the writer by a Luiseño informant as meaning my soul, "alma mia." Boscana, 317, gives pu-suni, his heart, as the San Juan Capistrano term for soul. The Sparkman Luiseño dictionary translates tolmal as a place in the center of the earth where some people go after death.

[22] In which they agree with almost all Indians.

San Juan Capistrano.[23]

We know that they adore a large bird similar to a kite, which they raise with the greatest care from the time it is young, and they hold to many errors regarding it.[24]

When a new moon shows itself they make a great outcry, which manifests their interest (negosijo). If there is an eclipse of the sun or of the moon, they shout with still louder outcries, beating the ground, skins, or mats with sticks, which shows their concern and uneasiness.[25]

San Gabriel.[26]

In this mission four distinct idioms are spoken according to the four directions of its establishment. One is called Kokomcar, another Guiguitamcar, the third Corbonamga, and the last Sibanga.[27]

---

[23] The Indians of San Juan Capistrano have sometimes been known as Juaneños. They speak a dialect similar to Luiseño. It is regarding them that the missionary Boscana has left the invaluable account that has been mentioned. The fathers in charge of San Juan Capistrano about 1811 were Francisco Suñer and Jose Barona.

[24] The large bird similar to a kite is no doubt the eagle or condor as among the Diegueño and Luiseño.

[25] The "outcry" at the appearance of the new moon is more fully described by Boscana. Racing by the young men formed a feature of the occasion. Boscana also mentions the concern felt at the time of an eclipse.

[26] The Indians of Mission San Gabriel were closely related in dialect to those of San Fernando. The two constituted a dialectic group which has been called the Gabrielino, and which is distinct from the other Shoshonean linguistic groups of Southern California. As will be seen, there were however other Indians at San Gabriel besides the true Gabrielino. The fathers in charge of this mission in 1811 were Jose de Miguel and Jose Maria Zalvidea.

[27] The four dialects spoken by the Indians assembled at this mission can be partially identified. Sibanga is the name of the site of San Gabriel itself. It is a local, not a tribal appellation, as is shown by the locative ending -nga. Hugo Reid in his account of the Indians of Los Angeles county, printed in the Los Angeles Star in 1852 and reprinted by Alexander Taylor in the California Farmer, gives Sibagna as the native name of San Gabriel. Guiguitamcar, or Guiquitamcar, is a good Spanish spelling of Gikidan-um, with the suffix -car substituted for the plural ending -um. Gikidanum is a variant obtained by the author for Gitanemuk, the name of the Shoshoneans on upper Tejon creek, at the southernmost end of the San Joaquin valley. These Indians speak a Serrano dialect. Their neighbors south of the Tehachapi range, that is towards San Gabriel, are also Serrano. A vocabulary of this dialect has been given in Volume IV of the present series of publications. The Kokomcar are unknown. The ending which this name shares with Guiguitamcar makes it seem that these people were also Serrano. Corbonamga is also unidentified. The ending may be the Gabrielino locative -nga. There is a possibility that either this term or the last is a copyist's misread spelling of the name Cucamonga.

Notwithstanding that in general they are ignorant of their origin, there have not been wanting some who declared that they had knowledge that the first Indians populating this country came from the north, whence they were conducted to these lands by a great chief (capitan general), who they say still exists on an island, and they make him be without beginning or end. This one distributed to each tribe its territory.[28]

When a celebrated captain dies, they summon the nearest villages, even if they are remote, and make a great festival, which consists of dancing and eating. They either bury the body, or burn it and bury its ashes. The dance and feast continue for a space of three days, after which the deceased remains in eternal oblivion.[29]

They are not acquainted with any other musical instrument than a whistle made from the bone of the foreleg of a deer, and a wooden fife (pifano).[30]

San Fernando.

The Indians of this mission speak three distinct tongues.[31]

The foods which they use are acorns; pine-nuts; chia (seeds of sage), called pasill in their language; islai, called chamiso by

---

[28] The great "capitan general" is no doubt the Gabrielino equivalent of the Juaneño and Luiseño deity Ouiot or Wiyot, who according to tradition led the people from the north and divided them into tribes.

[29] It is probable that cremation was the usual practice in pre-mission times. That the dead should be forgotten and their names never mentioned, is a universal custom of the California Indians. The accounts below from San Fernando and San Carlos give different explanations of the motive for the practice.

[30] The bone whistle is of the kind which may still occasionally be found in ceremonial use among the modern Indians of California. Many have been unearthed in archaeological explorations in Southern California. The "wooden fife" is no doubt the open-ended flute made by all the Indians of California, and more accurately described in the accounts from other missions below.

[31] While the Indians of San Fernando have been called Fernandeños or Fernandinos, their dialect was little different from that of San Gabriel, and the general term Gabrielino can be applied to both. There were also Serrano Indians at San Fernando. In fact it seems not unlikely that they may have been as numerous as the Gabrielino-speaking natives there. What the third language was which is mentioned as having been spoken at this mission, can only be conjectured. It is not unlikely that it was Chumash, for it is but a few miles westward from San Fernando to Chumash territory. The missionaries at San Fernando who might have written the present account were Martin de Landaeta, Jose Antonio Urresti, and Pedro Muñoz.

them; and numberless others. Of meat they eat deer, coyote, antelope, jackrabbit, rabbit, ground-squirrel, rat, dog, all birds, moles (topos), snakes, and rattlesnakes; and those of the coast are fond of all kinds of fish, especially whale.[32]

The musical instruments which they use are a flute of elder, certain little sticks, and whistles of deer bones.[33]

Nowadays they do not burn the dead as they did at the beginning of the conquest; but they do still put seeds with them at burial.

When an unconverted Indian dies, they make a deep hole for him. Into this they put a pot, a basket, an otter skin, and some two or three pesos worth of beads, above these the dead body, and this they cover with earth. Then they immediately give notice to all the villages of the district, that all, old, young, and children, are to paint for a general feast. In this feast every kind of seeds and meat is served, and the chief commands all most rigorously never to name the deceased, in order that he may not come to annoy them (arrastrarlos). Note: All should arrive weeping. At the end they burn the house and everything that the deceased possessed.

We have observed the following superstitions. In order that their faces may not be burned, they paint themselves with red ochre (almagre) and other colors. In order not to become tired in climbing hills, they carry a stick or stone. To hunt deer, they drink salt water and a plant which the Spanish call toloache and they manit. With this they intoxicate themselves. They take it in order to make themselves strong, to receive injury from nothing (tomer a nadie), that the rattlesnakes may not bite them, the bears not chew them, and that arrows may not enter their bodies.

---

[32] Chia, pasil, has been mentioned above. With "islai, called chamiso by them," compare R. S. Sparkman's "*Prunus ilicifolia*, Luiseño chamish, Spanish islaya." It is interesting that the bear is not given in the list of animals eaten. Many California Indians refrain from eating the bear on account of its human resemblance. Some did not eat the coyote, and those of northwestern California regarded dog meat as virulent poison.

[33] The "certain little sticks" may have been rattles made of a partly split stick, after the manner of a clap-stick. Such instruments were used by many California tribes to accompany dance songs.

According to information their gods are five and one goddess. They are called Veat, Taimur, Chuquit, Pichurut, and Iuichepet, husband of the goddess Manisar, and she is the one who gives them their seeds.[34]

The best known medicines are:

Vespibat.[35] This is composed of wild tobacco, lime, and oxide of iron (orinas) mixed together, which ferment. They take it to relieve themselves of pain in the stomach, as well as for wounds.

Chuchupate (an umbelliferous plant), called cayat in their language. This is a plant which on every stalk has three round leaves, each with a spike in the middle. The flower is white. They chew the root and rub themselves gently where they suffer pain. They also use it for headache.

With the anise plant they purge themselves.

With the herb called del pasmo (convulsion) they drive away toothache of the molars. When cooked they take it to sweat, and when crushed as snuff (como polvo de tabaco).

---

[34] Unfortunately the manuscript is not entirely clear. Chuquit may be read Chuguit or Chugerit. Iuichepet may be Inichepet or possibly Quichepet. On page 372 of the second volume of this series of publications is given a prayer, in the Yauelmani dialect of the Yokuts language, obtained from a man who had lived at Tejon, in intercourse with the Shoshonean Indians there. This prayer begins by calling on seven deities, whose names may be rendered, in untechnical orthography, Töushiut, Bamashiut, Yokhakhait, Echepat, Pitsuriut, Tsukit, and Ukat. Two or three of these terms look as if they might be Yokuts, but the etymology of none can be certainly explained in that language. The r in Pitsuriut is not found in Yokuts. At least part of these Yokuts terms therefore appear to have been borrowed from Shoshonean tribes. The names here given by the San Fernando father show the source of this borrowing. Chuquit of the San Fernando list is Yokuts Tsukit. Pichurut is Pitsuriut, and Iuichepet is Echepat. Veat is clear in the manuscript, but is probably intended for Vcat, that is, Ucat, with which the Yokuts Ukat would be identical. Taimur and the goddess Manisar have no Yokuts equivalents, and the three first names in the Yokuts list, Töushiut, Bamashiut, and Yokhakhait, do not occur among the San Fernando names. A distinction seems to exist among the Yokuts between these first three names and the borrowed four; for in a formula spoken in the Yokuts jimson-weed ceremony, given on the page following the prayer, only the first three are mentioned. The usual ceremonial number of the Yokuts is not seven but six, the number of the San Fernando deities. Ukat, the informant stated, was the sister of the others. A Serrano recently seen at San Manuel reservation in Southern California, mentioned six large stones that were once diosas, goddesses. These stones are at Nanamüvyat, in or near Little Bear Valley, but he had forgotten their names. The Yokuts correspondences make it more likely that the six San Fernando deities were Serrano than Fernandeño proper.

[35] The word vespibat is not otherwise known, but suggests pivat, tobacco, one of the components of the medicine.

Chilicote (*Echinocystis macrocarpa*), called yjaihix in the native language, they use mixed with dust of the stone called pafa, or paheasa in native dialect. They employ this for reducing inflammation, for driving away cataracts (nubes de los ojos), for wounds, to bring on menstruation, to cure themselves of urinary sickness, and boiled they take it to sweat (humederse).

Those who suffer from venereal humors, the syphilitic (convenerados), and the crippled, purge with mingled dust of alum stone and copperas (piedra alumbre y alcaparrosa).

When they feel heavy they bleed themselves with a flint.

When they are restless they refresh themselves with water from the bark of the ash tree.

When they suffer side pains they take red live ants in water, and apply them alive externally, and strike themselves with nettles.[35a]

They do not drink thermal waters, but they do bathe in them.

Among their principal diseases is syphilis (humor galico), of which a considerable number die. They are most often sick in the spring.

Santa Barbara.[36]

They bury the dead with all their pots and other poor jewels.[37]

[35a] Counter-irritants are not infrequently used by other Indians. The Mohave burn themselves with a glowing stick. Ants and nettles are used by the Luiseño and Juaneño as an ordeal in the initiation ceremonies for boys.

[36] With Santa Barbara the Shoshoneans are left behind, and the territory of the Chumash is entered. The missions of Santa Ynez and San Luis Obispo, as well as those of San Buenaventura and Purisima which are not here represented, were also in Chumash territory, and recruited chiefly from the Chumash Indians of the mainland and of the northern Santa Barbara islands. The fathers of Santa Barbara about the time this report was written were Luis Gil y Taboada and Marcos Amestoy.

[37] This is the first mission we have encountered where burial is the native mode of disposal of the dead. The practice continues as far as San Luis Obispo, after which cremation is again in practice as far as San Francisco, and in fact to the north of it beyond the sphere of mission influence. It is accordingly evident that the custom of cremation was distinctive of the Indians in the mission portion of the California coast, except only the Chumash. Archaeological investigations confirm the statements of early eye-witnesses. Numerous graves have been found in the Chumash region, but scarcely any in the regions to the north and south; except in certain layers of the shellmounds bordering San Francisco bay, in which region both cremation and burial seem to have been practised according to circumstances or period.—By "pots" are meant steatite vessels, not pottery, which has not been found so far north on the coast. The same explanation may apply to the "pots" mentioned above by the San Fernando informant.

They do not have chiefs (caziques), but in every village or town there are one or more who are called captains (capitanes). Not, however, that they have any authority over the rest, nor do these obey them or recognize them in any matter. Only he [is chief] who has charge of gathering the people when there is a prospect of a fight with another village, and to said chiefs the rest give beads at the dances or feasts which they sometimes make.

Santa Ynez.[38]

When the rancherias were still inhabited by unconverted Indians, there could be seen in various places bunches of feathers or plumes attached to sticks, which might be called their idol-temples (adoratorios). There they cast seeds and beads in order to obtain good harvests of acorns and other seeds which the fields produce of themselves, and which were their daily nourishment.

They neither knew or used any other musical instrument than a tube of wood resembling a flute, open at both ends and producing a buzzing quite disagreeable to hear; also a whistle (pito) of a limb-bone of some bird.

San Luis Obispo.

Fifteen different languages are spoken in this mission.[39]

I have found some wind instruments made of elder sticks.[40]

Notwithstanding that the Indians in their native state hold lands according to their families, there is no necessity of agreements to sow, as there are wild fruits on them; and if something

---

[38] The missionaries at Santa Ynez about 1811 or 1812 were Jose Antonio Calzada and Francisco Javier de Uria.

[39] The report on the Indians of San Luis Obispo was probably written by Father Luis Antonio Martinez. His companion, Antonio Rodriguez, did not come to San Luis Obispo until 1811. The San Luis Obispo Indians were Chumash, though the dialect of the vicinity of the mission differed markedly from those of Santa Barbara and Santa Ynez. It is difficult to conjecture what the fifteen languages mentioned can have been, unless they were slightly different dialects of Chumash. The number and distribution of the dialects of this family are very little known. It has been suspected that the dialects were numerous, and the present statement seems to be confirmatory. The only Indians other than Chumash likely to have been brought to San Luis Obispo, would be of the Salinan and Yokuts families.

[40] The wind instruments made of elder sticks are the flutes mentioned previously and again below.

rich is produced, it causes many wars if anyone has the boldness to go to collect the crop without previously paying or notifying the legitimate owner.[41]

There are all kinds (espiras or esleras), poor and rich, but among the rich there is in each village one to whom all look up and whose voice is respected by all such as are found living with him. To him, I do not know according to what rules, all offer tribute from their fruits, goods, and beads. Such men summon to the ceremonies all those who gather, and who are actually their friends. If by chance any one of these refuses the invitation, arms are resolved upon; and with the approval of his people the chief takes the road to avenge the injury which the other has done him by not accepting the invitation.[42] He deprives of life not only the chief but as many as are gathered with him. For all services they have no other reward than to look upon him, who has had the good fortune to kill some one, as a public person.

The Indians of each settlement or village have cemeteries marked out with boards or stones. They also have songs and ceremonies for burying the dead. They make a distribution of beads to all who have come together to assist in bringing the body to the grave. There is one, he who raises it on his back, who has for his particular duty the obligation of opening the grave. I have not been able to ascertain what their songs mean in our language.

---

[41] The translation has been given according to what appears to be the meaning of the text. This reads: Sin embargo de que los Indios tienen tierras por familias en su gentilidad, como son frutos silvestres no tienen necesidad de contratos, para sembrar, y si un objeto poderoso que produce, no pocas guerras, si alguno tiene el arrojo de ir à coger sus frutos sin pagar, y avisar, antes à su legitimo dueño.

[42] The statement that the rich man is the chief, is in accord with observations from almost all parts of California. The dependence of social rank on wealth seems, however, to have been greatest in this southern region and in northwestern California. The other missionaries contributing to this report make no mention of similar conditions. That the refusal of an invitation should cause war, seems also to indicate a greater influence and higher social position of the chief than among many California tribes. In most parts of the state it is very doubtful whether the inhabitants of one village would have been likely to commence war with those of a neighboring settlement merely on account of a slight put upon the dignity or prestige of their chief.

San Miguel.[43]

The neophytes at this mission speak four languages: that of San Antonio, which is reputed the principal one; that of the shore (la playana), which is the one spoken by those settled on the coast; the Tulareño; and another, that of the people of the south.[44]

The money of the Indians has been, and still is, beads, which they now lend without usury. In their wild state, usury consisted of the daily augmentation of the value of the amount lent, for instance a real of beads; and those who lent the real grew richer by as many reales as the original real was days in returning to their hands. This custom was practiced by those to the east of this mission.[45]

San Antonio.[46]

Two distinct languages spoken by the Indians are known: the predominant language, that of the site of the mission, which is understood to the east, south, and north and the circumference of the west; and the less important, which those speak who are called 'beach people' (playanos), on account of having come from the bays of the ocean. These are few in number, and not only understand the predominant language but also speak it perfectly.

They were as easily married as unmarried. For the former, nothing more was required than that the suitor should ask the

---

[43] San Miguel was in the territory of the Indians of the so-called Salinan stock. No general name of native origin is known for these people, who go under their present designation only because they lived in and about Salinas valley. The father who wrote the above reply was either Juan Martin or Juan Cabot.

[44] Of the four languages, the Tulareño is that of the people in the Tulare valley, namely the Yokuts. The people of the south are probably the most northwesterly Chumash, some of whom may have been brought to San Miguel instead of to San Luis Obispo. The language of San Antonio is Salinan, and that of the coast evidently so. Both are mentioned again in the replies from San Antonio. Nothing is known of the coast language of this region, nor about the dialectic divisions of the Salinan family, other than that the dialects ordinarily called those of San Miguel and San Antonio were somewhat different.

[45] No such custom of borrowing at interest has been otherwise reported from California.

[46] San Antonio is the northernmost of the two missions in Salinan territory. The missionaries there who might have contributed to this report were Pedro Cabot and Juan Bautista Sancho.

bride from her parents, and at times it sufficed that she of herself should consent to join herself to the man, though more often verbal communication or agreement (trato) preceded. Many of them did not keep their wives. Some, when their wife was pregnant or had given birth, changed their residence without taking leave, and married another. Others were married with two, three, or even more women. It is certain that there are many who have come [to the mission] from the mountains already married, and who could serve as an example to the most religious men.

There were some few who set out food for the dead.

From their native condition they still preserve a flute which is played like the dulce. It is entirely open from top to bottom, and is five palms in length. Others are not more than about three palms. It produces eight tones (puntos) perfectly. They play various tunes (tocatas), nearly all in one measure, most of them merry. These flutes have eleven [sic] stops; some more, and some less. They have another musical instrument, a string instrument, which consists of a wooden bow to which a string of sinew is bound, producing a note. They use no other instruments. In singing they raise and lower the voice to seconds, thirds, fourths, fifths, and octaves. They never sing in parts, except that when many sing together some go an octave higher than the rest. Of their songs most are merry, but some are somewhat mistes in parts. In all these songs they do not make any statement (proposicion), but only use fluent words, naming birds, places of their country, and so on.[47]

---

[47] The description of the flute accords well with specimens that have been collected from Indians of other parts of California, except that it is very doubtful whether any such flute could produce eight tones or had as many as eleven stops. The California flute ordinarily has either three or four stops. The ''string instrument'' is the musical bow, played with the mouth as a resonance chamber, and reported also from the Maidu and Yokuts. When it is said that some sing an octave higher than others when they sing together, it is probable that women are meant. The use of disjointed words or names, many times repeated in songs, is frequent in California. On the other hand there are instances of songs containing several complete sentences, as among the Yokuts songs published in Volume II of this series.

San Carlos.[48]

At this mission there are seven nations of Indians. They are called Excelen and Egeac, Rumsen, SargentaRuc, Sanconeños, Guachirron and Calendo Ruc. The first two are from inland. They have one and the same language or speech, but this is totally distinct from that of the other five, who speak a common tongue.[49]

In the native state they ordinarily lived at war with one another.

---

[48] The mission of San Carlos, near Monterey, is so far as known the only one to which Indians of the Esselen family were brought, except perhaps that of Soledad. San Carlos is one of seven missions, extending from Soledad to San Francisco, founded in Costanoan territory. The following report, which is one of the most detailed and careful in the entire series of replies, appears to have been written either by Father Juan Amoros or by Father Vincente de Sarria.

[49] The seven "nations" are village communities. On account of unusual size or prominence, the names of these seem to have come to be chosen to designate somewhat larger groups that had no political organization or real coherence except possibly a distinct dialect. The first two, "from inland," who have the same speech, distinct from that of the others, belong to the Esselen family; the other five, who "speak a common tongue," are Costanoan. Excelen is evidently the same name as Esselen, which appears also in the forms Eslen, Ecclemach, Ecselen, Escelen, and Ensen. Originally probably only the name of a village-site, extended by the Spaniards to cover a group of people, it has come to be the recognized name of an entire linguistic family. This family was never large since known to history, and is the only stock in California to have become entirely extinct. However, only the lives of a few individuals separate several other families from the same condition, so that there is nothing peculiar in the fate of the Esselen. Egeac is the Ekgiagan given by Alexander Taylor as a village of the Chalone of Soledad, who, however, were Costanoan; -gan seems to be an ending, as it appears also in Eslanagan, Yumanagan, and Aspasniagan. The writer in 1902 was told by the Costanoan Indians at Monterey that Ekkheya was a former village-site in the mountains to the south. This accords with what is known of the Esselen territory. Rumsen or Rumsien is the name which has come to be used for the Costanoan Indians of the vicinity of Monterey. The few survivors state that it was applicable to the people, or a district, along Carmel river in the mountains south of Monterey. Rumsen and Eslen are the most commonly mentioned "tribes" at Monterey, which have by some, writing at a distance, been extended so as to divide a large part of California between them. In this more general sense they are about equivalent to "Costonoan and Esselen Indians at San Carlos mission." SargentaRuc is Sirkhintaruk, or Sirkhinta, also called Kakonta, a former Costanoan village at Point Sur. Kakon means chicken-hawk; ta is the locative ending *at*; and ruk, literally house, means village, or people of; or, as the writer's informants put it, Kakonta is Sur, Kakontaruk the Sureños, the "gente" of Sur. Guachirron is several times mentioned, as by Taylor, who speaks of the Goatcharones with the Ekgiagan. The writer's Monterey informants placed the Huacharones beyond Ekkheya. Calendo Ruc, finally, is Kalindaruk, a Costanoan village near the mouth of Salinas river. Like most the other terms in this list, it has generally been used to include the people of the surrounding district. Kalin is ocean, ta is at, and ruk, house, as in Sirkhintaruk. The name has also been written Calendaruc and Kathlendaruc.

The languages which there are among these seven nations are two, one called Rumsen, and the other Excelen, entirely different. For instance in Rumsen they say, muxina muguiant jurriquimo igest oyh laguan eje uti maigin. In Excelen, egenoch lalucuimxs talogpami ege salegua lottos tahezapami laxlachis. Both of these examples mean: "The men who shoot well with a bow are esteemed and well liked."[50]

The principal Indians are their chiefs or kings. Each nation has one. They obey and respect him all their lives. The position is inherited by succession, or in case of want of direct succession it goes to the nearest relative. In the native condition such a captain was the only one in his nation who could have and leave various unmarried women. If he had children from any one of them, she was the best beloved and he lived with her forever. However he had the privilege of going with unmarried women whenever he desired. The whole nation rendered him vassalage. He went ahead in war, furnishing bows and arrows and animating his people. He was regularly an excellent marksman with the bow.

There is a custom among the men of entering daily a subterranean oven which is called temescal. Into this they bring fire. When it is sufficiently heated, they go in undressed. Then they sweat profusely, so that when they come out they look as if they had been bathing. It is known that this is very beneficial to them. For some time the [sweat-houses] were forbidden, and many itches, tumors, and other epidemics were found among the men. On the [sweat-houses] being given back to them, hardly a

---

[50] The Esselen language is extinct. All that is known of it is collected in a paper on the Languages of the Coast of California South of San Francisco, issued in the second volume of the present series of publications. The sentence here added is therefore a welcome contribution, even though it does not yet yield to analysis. Egenoch is man and lottos arrow, according to the vocabularies. The mx in lalucuimxs is doubtful in the manuscript, also the g in ege, and the z in tahezapami, for which taherapami should perhaps be read. The Costanoan dialect of San Carlos and Monterey has been briefly discussed, under the name of Rumsen, in the publication just mentioned. Mukiamk is man, uti is they, ekhe is much, very, lauwan is bow, ius or iwis, not discernible in the sentence above, is like, love, tepek, also without parallel, is to shoot; -st and -n are verbal endings. Igest should perhaps be read iyest, and the end of maigin is not clear in the manuscript.

man with the itch could be discovered, and this is a disease common among the women and children, who do not use such sweat-baths. The women who have recently given birth employ another method of sweating. They make a hole inside of the house, put wood into it, light this, and put many heavy stones upon it. When the stones are hot, they cover them with much green verdure which makes a sort of a mattress. The woman who has given birth lies down on this with the baby. The mother sweats much and the child is kept warm.[51] They do this for six or seven days, and then are as agile as if they had not given birth, and this although their broths and foods are very poor.

They use a split stick like a distaff which serves them to beat the measure for their songs,[52] which, whether happy or sad, are all in the same time (tonata). For instance they sing as follows to the lively tunes, in which they mention their seeds or their asañas: *Bellota—a—a, bellota; mucha semilla—a—a, mucha semilla.* If the song is one of vengeance or bad wishes, which is very often, and from which many fights result, they sing, and dance to the same time, speaking evil of that nation with which they are on bad terms, thus: *Manco—o—o, manco,* or other words or defects which they know concerning the nation or person which they are comparing (contrapuesta).

The kind of idolatry which has been found among these natives is that they sometimes smoke, blowing the smoke to the sun, the moon, and to certain people who they believe live in the sky; and with this they say: "Here goes this smoke in order that you will give me good weather to-morrow." Thus also of the seeds which they gather and of which they make pinole or flour. Of these they throw a handful to the sun, the moon, or the sky, saying: "I send you this so that another year you will give me greater abundance." Thus they recognize in the sun and the

---

[51] This method of sweating used by women who have recently given birth, suggests the Luiseño and Diegueño practice at the girls' puberty ceremony, as described by Boscana and in an article by H. N. Rust in the American Anthropologist for 1906.

[52] The split stick is the clap-stick or rattle that has been previously mentioned. It is the dancing rattle of central California, as compared with the cocoon rattle used by the shamans of the same tribes.

moon influences bearing upon their necessities, and recognize also that in the sky there is another people which sends them what they wish, and for this reason they offer them flour, seeds, and tobacco smoke.

They have often been asked if they have heard tell anything of the place of their origin. To this all answer that they do not know. And this ignorance is not strange, for these natives hold it for the greatest affront that one should speak of their dead parents and relatives; to such a degree, that a boy whose parents should die while he is quite small, would have no one who would tell him how his deceased father, grandfather, and other kindred were called.[53] If they quarrel among one another, they say in order to be more vituperative: "Your father is dead (a ti se te murio tu padre)" and then they become more angry.[54] On account of these practices they have no way of retaining a recollection of their ancestors, the more so since when anyone dies, they burn all his clothing and property, and if he has animals, like chickens, dogs, or a horse, they kill them, and pull up his plants. If they are asked the reason, they say that it is in order that they may no longer remember the dead.[55]

Some of them gain a reputation as a doctor (curandero). The sick person calls such a one and lets him suck the part which is paining. Presently the doctor extracts a stone which he has hidden in his mouth, and says: "Look. This was the cause of your sickness. Inside of you was this stone." They receive pay for this deceit and the patient does not become well from it. Others sing and dance before the sick person. Others, old women, say that it is they who make fruits and seeds grow, and for this presents are made to them; and if by chance the year is barren in fruits, the old woman pretends that she is angered, making

---

[53] This might be literally true.

[54] Some such statement is the usual form which a deadly insult or curse takes among the California Indians, from the Yurok of the extreme northwest to the Mohave of the southeast.

[55] The reason here given for the destruction of the property of the dead, and the avoidance of his name, is the one usually obtained upon inquiry among the present Indians of California. That there were also other motives, appears from the preceding statement from San Fernando. The matter has been discussed in Notes on California Folk-Lore in the Journal of American Folk-Lore for 1906.

them believe that she has not wished to give them fruits; wherefore they feel themselves compelled to make her more presents in order to allay her displeasure and make her give them seeds the next year. If indeed this next year is a fruitful one, the old woman receives their contentment and approval and all humor her.

San Juan Bautista.[56]

They say that the first Indians to settle this country came from the north after a great flood;[57] that some went back and did not return; and that here sprung the single common language which is spoken in the seven missions about here, although somewhat changed [from place to place.]

They did not have chiefs. The bravest and strongest were those who went out to their wars. Every man acted as he wished.

Santa Cruz.[58]

At this place they ordinarily live on salmon and lampreys, of which there are many in the river which flows at the mission.[59]

Their dances are most insipid. They gather in a circle and without moving from the spot bend their bodies. They move their feet and make many contortions to the sound of their disagreeable voices, with which they do not form articulate words.

---

[56] The mission of San Juan Bautista is farthest inland of those in Costanoan territory. The dialect of San Juan Bautista, named Mutsun after a village near the mission, is known from a grammar and phrase-book prepared by Father Felipe Arroyo de la Cuesta, who is probably the author of the following replies, as he was at San Juan Bautista at the time the report was called for.

[57] That the Indians of this region believed in a great flood or primeval water, is corroborated by such information as there is in existence about their mythology. That they had a tradition of a migration from the north seems more doubtful, not so much because there is any positive information to the contrary, as that the most careful inquiries among nearly all the surviving tribes of central California have failed to reveal the existence of any migration legends or historical traditions. See the introduction to a collection of Indian myths of south central California, published in the fourth volume of the present series.

[58] The following was probably written by Father Andreas Quintana. Santa Cruz is in Costanoan territory, and so far as known was settled only with Indians of this family.

[59] Salmon and lampreys, ordinarily known as eels, were the most important aboriginal fish foods of northern California.

There are some among them, evil-minded old men, who instill them with a panic fear towards the demon whom they regard as the author of all evil.[60] That he may not trouble them, they make them believe that they must place a little of the flour which they eat, or of any other of their foods, on this stone or in that log in such and such a place. For the same purpose they sometimes hold secret dances at night, always without the knowledge of the fathers. It is known that at night the adult men alone gather in a field or wood. In the middle they place a tall stick crowned with a bundle of tobacco leaves, or branches of trees or other plants. At the foot of the stick they put their foods and glass beads. They prepare for the dance, tornandose their bodies and faces. When they are all gathered, the old man whom they look up to as their master or soothsayer goes out to give ear to the commands of the devil. Returning after a short time, he imparts to the poor innocents, not what he op [sic] of the father of lies, but what his own perversity and malice suggest to him. Thereupon they proceed to their dance, which they continue until day.

When an Indian wishes to marry, he goes to the house of her whom he desires for a wife and seats himself near her, sighs without speaking a word, and throwing at the feet of her father some beads,—which are small snails or pieces of shells strung on a thread—he goes out and without further ceremony or rite he is married.

Generally they are peaceful. They do not give quarter to the enemy. When one of these is killed in battle, they tear his limbs to pieces. They remove the top of the skull,[61] place it on a pike (pica), carry it in triumph to their village, y la pasean por todas las de sus abiados.

---

[60] The ''demon who is the author of all evil'' is of course a missionary conception, as are the ''perversity and malice'' attributed to the head man of the dances.

[61] Many of the California Indians did not scalp, but cut off the head or the skin of the entire head except the face.

Santa Clara.[62]

There are three languages at this mission, two of them related (bastante parecidos), and the third, which is of the east, totally distinct.

Sometimes they bury the dead, sometimes burn them.[63] As to whether they place food with them, we believe that they do not.

They do not know any distinction of superiority. Only in war do they obey the chief, and the wizards and magicians in matters of superstition. In everything else everyone does what he pleases. In their dissensions and disputes the strongest party wins.

San Jose.[64]

Only in war do they obey the most valiant or successful one, and in matters of superstition their wizards and magicians. Beyond this they admit no civil, political, nor even domestic subordination. In their quarrels they have no appeal, except to force, whence it follows that even those of the same family sometimes kill one another for nothing at all.[65]

It is said that only one village or nation, of the many that composed the population of this mission, adored the sun when it retired to the southern pole. They considered it angered, made a dance for it, and offered it seeds, until they knew that it had turned and was again approaching.

---

[62] Santa Clara is in Costanoan territory, but it is probable that Miwok or Yokuts Indians were brought here as they were brought to San Jose and San Juan Bautista. It is in this way that the third and totally distinct language mentioned is to be explained. The missionaries at Santa Clara in 1811 were Magin Catalá and Jose Viader.

[63] It would appear from the San Francisco account below, and from other evidence, that burning was the more customary.

[64] Mission San Jose, which was not at the present city of San Jose, but some distance to the north, was in Costanoan territory, but included in its population Indians of the Miwok and perhaps other families. Nearly all of the few descendants of the Indians once at this mission are Miwok. Fathers Buenaventura Fortuni and Narciso Duran were at San Jose in 1811.

[65] It looks as if this passage and the preceding paragraph from Santa Clara had had a common origin.

San Francisco.[66]

At this mission there were five languages.[67]

When married people separate, the children regularly follow the mother.

As soon as a person has stopped breathing, if he has few relatives or lazy ones, they bury him. Those who have friends or relatives who will bring wood, are burned. The little property that they have, and some few seeds, they burn with them, which is the more usual practice.

May 11, 1907.

---

[66] San Francisco was the most northerly of the missions in Costanoan territory, and in fact the most northerly of the Franciscan missions in California except that of San Rafael. The missionaries in charge in 1811 were Ramon Abella and Juan Saenz de Lucio.

[67] The five languages of this mission may have been the dialects of the five Costanoan tribes mentioned in Schoolcraft as gathered at this mission: Olhon, Ahwaste, Altahmo, Romonan, Tulomo.

CPSIA information can be obtained at www.ICGtesting.com
Printed in the USA
LVOW11s0310200114

370096LV00001B/38/P

9 781162 930954